Poems of Gitanjali

POEMS
OF
GITANJALI

ORIEL PRESS
STOCKSFIELD
BOSTON   HENLEY   LONDON

© Khushi Badruddin 1982

First published in 1982
by Oriel Press Ltd.
(Routledge & Kegan Paul Ltd.)
at Branch End, Stocksfield
Northumberland, NE43 7NA

Reprinted 1982

Printed and bound in England
by Knight & Forster, Leeds

ISBN 0 85362 195 0 *Hard Cover*
202 7 *Paperback*

Designed by Bruce Allsopp.
Cover design by Dalma Flanders

CONTENTS

ACKNOWLEDGEMENTS

*Publication of this book has been supported
by Camellia Investments Ltd.*

*The publishers are deeply grateful to Pritish Nandy
for his initiatives, perception and help in many ways.*

*Above all, we thank Gitanjali's mother, Mrs
Badruddin, without whose dedicated care in finding
and transcribing the poems this publication would not
have been possible. She has helped us in many ways
and by her wish all royalties will go to charities in
India.*

FOREWORD

The fact that she was called Gitanjali, after the book of Rabindranath Tagore, perhaps predisposed her to poetry, to a philosophical vision of the world, to a completely modest sense of her own importance. Whether this beautiful child ever contemplated the possibility that her poems would be published we do not know. There are indications in the poems themselves that she may have done, a feeling that they would come out of the hiding places she contrived for them and carry her essence beyond her physical death. That somehow these poems were *meant* to be published has been felt by all of us who have been involved in producing this volume. Each of us may have interpreted this feeling differently but in one way or another we were all moved in the same direction. In his introduction, the distinguished poet, Pritish Nandy, has used the word miraculous: all of us are aware of a remarkable series of events and personal relationships which now culminate in the publication. It took quite a long time, as one might expect.

Khushi Badruddin, Gitanjali's mother, began the collection of the hidden poems. She failed to interest people who might have published some of them and, in desperation, aimed above her wildest hopes in sending them to *The Illustrated Weekly of India* where Pritish Nandy was profoundly moved by them. He describes in his Introduction how Gordon Fox became aware of the poems and a prime mover in their publication.

My own involvement came when David Bacon, a friend and colleague of Gordon Fox and a director of

Oriel Press, asked me to look at Gitanjali's poems. I thought they were marvellous and I wrote as follows.

I have now read all Gitanjali's poems. They are beautiful, deeply moving and at times I had to stop reading because my eyes were full of tears. But these poems transcend sorrow. Their power does not come from their being a record of suffering by a young and beautiful girl condemned to a lingering death by a painful and humiliating disease. That, alas, is all too common. Gitanjali prayed that she might live up to her name which is the title of Tagore's first book of poems and means *song-offering*. She did. She was given the wisdom of great simplicity, a faultless ear for the meaningful music of words and direct communion with God.

The religious poems, personally addressed to God, are remarkable in their objectivity. They are not mystical and they are free from any corruption of creed or doctrine. They speak to and for all people who believe in God, whatever their particular religion may be, and could give offence to nobody except a fanatical materialist. Likewise, at the human level of personal loves and relationships, Gitanjali universalises the particular. The poem which touched me most deeply is MOTI MY FRIEND, which is a crystalline expression of the anguish of being prevented by illness from serving a fellow being who has become dependent.

Some of Gitanjali's prayers were granted, some were not and she understood what had to be. She did not ask *why?* — the perilous reiterated question which has led our world to the brink of ruin, and there is in her poetry a quality of wisdom which has its roots in the East and is needed in the West.

It was agreed that Oriel Press would publish the

poems and there was a special, if poignant, coincidence in that Frances and David Bacon were grieving for their younger son, Nicky, a most talented and maturely dedicated boy who, like Gitanjali, died at the age of sixteen.

Feeling as I did, and do, the intense beauty and innocence of the poems, I had the editorial problem that, in a few places, the language was used in slightly unusual ways. There were inconsistencies in the use of capital letters and in punctuation, which might be regarded as blemishes, but I felt that, for Gitanjali, they were meaningful, so it was decided to publish the poems as they were written and treat them with all the respect due to the work of a true poet.

There was a suggestion by Mrs Badruddin that this volume might be dedicated to her son, Gitanjali's beloved brother, but this is a posthumous publication. It is implicitly dedicated to her family and, as the response to Pritish Nandy's publication of a few of the poems has shown, to all who have died young and those who have grieved for them.

Bruce Allsopp,
Oriel Press,
Stocksfield. 1982.

INTRODUCTION

by
Pritish Nandy

I first came across Gitanjali's poems when I was editing the poetry page of *The Illustrated Weekly of India,* the largest circulation magazine in the land, which seemed to attract every single wordsmith around. As a result I was always flooded with verse of all kinds and irate letters from those I would not publish. Among a large number of poems that reached me one evening, I found a sheaf sent by Khushi Badruddin. M. V. Kamath, who was then Editor, had forwarded them to me in Calcutta, saying that Mrs Badruddin had personally come and left these poems for me. These were the offerings of a girl of sixteen: Gitanjali.

I was curious. I read through the poems first, and then went back to read Khushi Badruddin's little note attached to them. It explained that she found these poems several months after Gitanjali, her only daughter, died of cancer. They were hidden under the mattress; in little corners of her room; behind books, sofa seats; inside cushion covers; wherever she could reach out and conceal them. The reason was apparent. Gitanjali knew she was terminally ill but she did not want her mother to know this. She did not want to hurt her.

She suffered quietly. In the loneliness of her room at home and at the hospital (she journeyed from one to the other every few days as her sick body faltered and recovered from time to time) she tried to come to terms with her fate. These poems lend voice to that suffering, to that intense loneliness. And yet, what is remarkable, is that there is no sense of despair. There is only the quiet dignity of one who has learnt to live with hurt.

That is what appealed to me.

I published an entire page of Gitanjali's poems. I was sure they would touch a cord somewhere. What I was not quite prepared for was the incredible response. The offices of the weekly were swamped with letters from thousands of readers. Everyone was moved by Gitanjali's poems; many had similar stories to tell, of children who showed immense courage before death, who showed love and understanding few of us would dare in such circumstances. It was absolutely amazing.

Since then, Khushi Badruddin and I have met. She told me how Gitanjali loved to write and paint and watch the sea outside her window. She told me how strong her will to live was, and how she grappled with her illness for months till her weak body, racked by pain, finally succumbed. There was never any self-pity, no horror of the ultimate dark. Only a quiet acceptance of pain and sorrow, an implicit faith in God and an awareness of the fact that whatever was happening to her was beyond anyone's control.

These poems of Gitanjali may not have been meticulously crafted. You could fault them on form or literary style. But does that really matter? Does it matter whether Gitanjali could write a perfect sonnet or not? What moves me in these poems is the simplicity of her language, the honesty and the anguish with which she speaks and asks questions of her God. That is why these poems are so beautiful. That is why they reach out to so many people.

Many of the questions Gitanjali asks can never be answered. Perhaps there are no answers you and I can give. Why should a beautiful childhood suddenly falter? Why should such unbearable agony come upon those who have never hurt anyone? Is sorrow our ultimate destiny in this imperfect universe?

I don't know.

All I know is this: these poems have hurt me by an awareness I would like to share with others. The miracle of pain that opens up worlds we never knew existed.

Even this book is a miracle.

Ever since the poems first appeared, Khushi Badruddin and I were keen that all Gitanjali's poems should be collected and put together with a brief introductory note explaining how they were discovered. In fact, new poems were always being found: inside books; carefully kept away in the pockets of old, discarded skirts; hidden behind the toys in the almirah; unfinished drafts crumpled and thrown into attic corners. We were wondering what to do with all these poems, which publisher to appeal to, when I suddenly received a 'phone call from someone speaking on behalf of Gordon Fox.

Of course, I had heard of Gordon Fox. Anyone in Calcutta who knows anything about the tea business would have heard of Gordon Fox. But what did he want to speak to me about? Publishing. Publishing what? My poems? No, he was wondering if you would like to discuss a book of poems by Gitanjali. But Gitanjali has no book of poems. That's what Mr Fox was wondering. Can we bring out a book of poems by Gitanjali?

That's how this book began.

Several months later, when I met Gordon Fox in Bombay — I had flown over from Calcutta to meet him and return the same evening — he solved the riddle. He told me how he first discovered Gitanjali's poems. And that, too, was a strange story. He was in Bombay on one of his regular visits. Strolling back to his hotel near Apollo Bunder, where the sea quietly catches the colours of the dusk, he found a torn sheet of paper, wind-blown, at his feet. He casually picked it up. Someone had wrapped something in it and then thrown the wrapping away.

It was the page of the weekly on which I had published Gitanjali's poems.

That is when Gordon Fox traced me all the way to Calcutta; that is how this book was first conceived. Since then, we have all been working on it. Gordon Fox, Bruce Allsopp, Khushi Badruddin and I, hoping to bring out a book that will convey Gitanjali's courage to thousands of people all over the world.

For those who have personally known Gitanjali, this book will bring back beautiful memories of a child who loved life deeply, despite all her wounds. And for others, who did not know her but have perhaps known others who suffered the same plight, I am sure Gitanjali's poems will offer them an insight into the courage all children are capable of when faced with the dark of the unknown.

Despite our different gods, our different perceptions of life and truth, each of us walk the same way. Poems like Gitanjali's occasionally light up the darkness and show us that all sorrow is universal. Just as love is.

Pritish Nandy

Calcutta
15th May 1982

GITANJALI

Born in Meerut on 12th June 1961
Died in Bombay on 11th August 1977

I am named

GITANJALI

After the famous book of Tagore
I wish and pray
Oh! help me God
I so live that . . .
I live up to the name.

THE GLORY OF THE SUN

Every evening
When
The day
Meets
The dusk
I sit
In my window
And watch
The sinking sun.

When
The light fades away
Slowly
And
The hours
Grow
Quiet and lonely
My heart too
Sinks
Within my soul.

For
I know not
If
I will see
The glory
Of...
The sun again.

PRESENCE OF GOD

There's a presence of God
In every thing
We don't really know
When and where
That moment shall come
Or in which form
He may appear.

Therefore
Speak not in vain
Cause no one pain
Spread what ever little
Happiness you can
Give a helping hand
And when you find
Friend or foe
Smile . . .
For who knows
You may heal or mend
A broken heart
And make your foe a friend.

THEIR EYES HELD NO PROMISE

The night
Of the storm
Held me
In the grip of fear.

It was not so much
The storm that I feared
It was the
Over-whelming emotions
The sinking feeling
Of two loving souls
That held me close
To their heart.

It was not so much
My own pain and suffering
But their blood-drained
Faces that stared
Into the space.

Their eyes held no promise
And looked beyond me
Not once daring
To meet my
Dying probing eyes.

Not that I am proud
Not that I am a non-believer
But I long stopped begging
For mercy.

Looking up at their faces
Who try to hide their
Pain and sorrow.

4

I am sorry for their sake
And not for myself
At least dear God
I plead with you
Either put an end
To this wick of candle
Or let it glow steadily
For a few years more.

LITTLE NOTES OF LOVE

Most of the nights
When
The world at large
Is asleep
I lie awake
In the dark and try
Not to weep
Mercy I cry
Mercy Oh God
Have mercy upon me
Allow my wounded heart
And my wounds to heal
Dare I ask
Oh my God
What have I done
To deserve this
Where Oh where
Those happy days are gone
Where Oh where
And why? Oh God
My friends
Like Candy are gone
"Get well soon"
"Cheer-up" is all
The mail-man brings
Strange eyes, very strange
But it's the warmth of these
"Little notes of love"
That helps my feeble heart to tick.

IN THE DEEP SILENCE OF THE NIGHT

I keep waiting
For you to come
I love
The moments
We spent together
I call out to you
In the deep silence
Of the night.
Oh, Please come
Just once before...
I forever rest.

Tears and sleeplessness
Have played their part
In lending
The heaviness
To my eyes.

I have no anchor
I am drifting
All the time
I cannot anymore
Hide my grief
I wish
I could wail
My sorrow
From the house-tops
Do please come
Just once.

How can I bring
My aching heart to rest
I am only waiting
For death to sting.

SLEEP

Sleep,
When did we meet last?
You and I
Seem to have become strangers.
Once not long ago
You were so close to me;
You would enfold me and
Take me by my hand
To escort me
To the distant hills
And help me build
Castles in my dreams.
Now it all seems so strange;
I only remember you so vaguely.

Remember how once we shared
Some tendermost thoughts?
Now I am left
With memories alone,
Sometimes some word rings
To revive our past . . .
Like a lullaby,
A goodnight kiss
Reminds me of that
Beautiful thing
Called sleep.
And now I lie staring at the dark,
Lonesome and sad.

Once in a way
Sleep
Overtakes me
And then the dreams
Seem so far away.

8

ALAS

An oil lamp
Wearily burns
Beside my bed
Where I lay down
My head to rest.

I see the misery
On the faces
Hovering around me,
Not knowing when
Death might strike.

I whom death
Awaits to claim
Am not afraid.
I will welcome her
With open arms.
Alas,
There are only tears to offer
In relief and
My wasted form.

MEMORIES ARE ALL THAT I HAVE

Each morning
When I greet
The world
My heart swells up
And my eyes fill with tears.

As I take in
The past and the present
The time stands still
For a while
From the spring-board
Of my memory
Many thoughts
Dive into my mind
Some are happy,
Some are painfully sad
These memories are all that I have
I live on them
I feast and depend on them
I could die . . .

Did I say die?
Oh no! No dear God
Please let me live
Hold me tight my mother dear
Do not let me sink
Into the depths of my woes
I promise
Never to speak in despair again.

Although
I've been through
The deepest sorrow
Deeper pain and grief
And yet . . .
I beg of you dear God
"Please let me live".

My tears flow silently
Fast and free
My bruised heart
Murmurs faintly
And I make a promise brave
Never to indulge
In self-pity again.

I raise my weary eyes
To catch a glimpse
Of the fading Day-Star
Hoping
He will come again
To greet me
And warm up
My shattered heart.

Published in FEMINA Nov. 23-Dec. 7, 1979

11

I BESEECH YOU

I seek you God
In my prayers,
I seek you God
Everywhere
I seek you
In the rising sun,
I seek you
When the day is done.
I seek you even
When I dream and drift,
I seek you
For your healing touch
When I am in pain,
And wish so much to thank you
When you take the pain away.

I seek you in my mother
And
In my father too,
I seek your guidance
In all I say and do.
And if perchance
I fail to be good
And take your name in vain
Please God understand
For I am so much in pain.
I thank you
For those few rare moments
When you make me laugh
Though in pain,
I cherish those moments
Like a treasure
And live on the happy
Memories you gave.

I feel your presence
In my mother
And
In my father's clasp
And I am sure
You know that
I seek nothing
Save the truth.
In you lies the truth
And, therefore,
I seek you.

I shall seek you most
At my hour of death
And I beseech you
My dear God
To be by my side
And hold my hand
And take me
Where you want.

With child-like faith
I cling to this hope;
So please have mercy
And come to me.

MY PETS

Micky, Judy and I
We've been long together
Through pleasant and
Through cloudy weather
Such joyful memories
I have of our plays
Inside, today
My heart weeps away

But I keep mum
For fear of hurting
Those who love me
And feel with-me-one

Micky and Judy
Whine and howl
And wonder why
I am so indifferent and quiet

They little thought
It thus could be
Their friend so full of fun and games
Is silently slipping away

If only they knew
And understood my plight
They would weep their heart out
Day and night
They wag their tails
They lick my hand
And try their best
To cheer me if they can.

Published in *Eve's Weekly*, Feb 10–16, 1979

14

OH DEATH TREAD SOFTLY

Oh death
I have such
Mixed feelings
For you
Sometimes
I dread you
Sometimes
I await thee
I know not
When
Thou shall embrace me

Oh, death
I do have a favour to ask thee
When thou comest
Oh, please dear death
Do come but
Unannounced
For there are crushed hearts
Within these walls
Hearts that love, adore and care
Hearts that bleed
Inwardly
And show not a care
But they do care
For the one
Whom you await to claim
Let them be asleep
Or take me in my slumber
For partings are so painful
Especially for those
Who reared me . . .
From a seeding to a flower

15

Oh death
Tread softly
For I fear for those
Who fear for me
Do not be very harsh
Spare me, oh please spare me
Little suffering
Spare me a little pain
And please spare me just a . . .
Few tears
To shed them
In the presence of God
To show HIM my gratitude
For after all isn't HE
Sparing me
From this cruel, cruel world
Where there are
Some people
Who don't even have a heart.

Published in *Eve's Weekly*, Feb. 10–16, 1979

MY MOTHER

She is like a pillar of strength
To, all, each one and sundry
She radiates the warmth
Even when she passes by
She showers the
Blessings through her
Lullabye

The emotions overwhelm her
The tears flow silently
And yet the eyes smile
And blink a message
Of love and understanding

I hold my breath (in pain no doubt)
And look up in amazement
And try my utmost best
And slowly and silently I
Close my eyes; With Thine
Expression to cool my own

I once wondered how it
Thus could be
A frail soul could bear
The brunt of life smilingly
But it seeped through me
Like water through the plant
That no matter what may come
You've got to fight the weedlings
For the survival of your young

With sadness weighing heavily
In the precious eyes

That I adore
She creeps silently and softly
Into the little den
Which is my very own

She looks upon me
With love brimming in her eyes
And reaches out to ease me
When fever's burning me inside

Her eyes
Mirror the reflection of love
The sadness of her withered heart
The pain of the gone-by years

And in those eyes
I seek and find
The friendly glow of confidence
That pulls me up
When all else fails
Including the hand of God.

The strong wind blew
The clouds clapped their hands
I shuddered and clung to my
Faith in that hand.

Published in *Eve's Weekly*, Feb. 10–16, 1979

I AM WALKING ALONE

Tonight, as on other nights
I'm walking alone
through the valley of fear.
O God, I pray
that you will hear me:
for only you alone know
what is in my heart.
Lift me out of this valley of despair
and set my soul free.

I try to lift my soul so high
that nothing can touch it
where it lies . . .
Bruised and crushed
lies my trust, faith and soul.

When my hour comes
I will not be afraid . . .
for I know
Your judgement will be
tempered with mercy.
After all I am only clay
And one day
I shall return . . .
To the dust
From which I came.

MY PRAYERS

I often pray fervently
To Almighty God
Whispering and sending my prayers above
In vain I beg, in vain I implore
Oh! God please make me well soon
And let me go back to school
I miss my friends and all the fun

I shall wait and see
But will beg no more
Neither for my sake nor
For my mother's
If that's how you wish
If that's how you want
"THY WILL BE DONE".

Lucky are those
Who go to slumber
I lie awake — in the dark and stumble . . .
Over the bitter sweet memories
Of my childhood . . .

Sometimes I am at a loss
To think about life
And the life here after
I dread the thought of parting
And bidding a good-bye
And yet
I am brave enough
To face —
Even death
When it comes by-and-by.

Published in *Eve's Weekly*, Feb. 10–16, 1979

ECHOES OF MY PAST

Once there lurked
A desire
Silently in my heart
To be alone
Which is most unlike me
I went to the sea-side
To be with my thoughts for a while
The silence was so heavy
So suffocating
All was quiet around me
Except within my heart
It's a strange kind of disturbance
The rocks
Look lonesome
And sad like me
Only I am frail and weak
And they stand
Majestically strong
How I envy them
My thoughts
Carry me away
Like a tide
Suddenly
I hear a child crying in distance . . .
The soothing sound of the consoler
Is strangely familiar
I hear a giggle mingled with tears and sob
How strange it all seems
I suppose
They are the echoes of my past.
The sinking Sun
Does little to lift my low morale
Alas
I am more sad

And heavy of heart
I dont know
How long I stood thus
Deep in my thoughts
Suddenly
I am alone no more
My dog Micky
Stood at my feet
Licking away my wounded heart
He looked up sadly
And wagged his tail
Pleading for a pat and a smile
My weary smile did help a little
For he was soon happily chasing
The gulls on the rocks
I once more
Was carried away
By the tide of my thoughts
Micky barked
And once again
Tore me from
My painful chain of thoughts.

The calm of the sea
Was replaced by the roar
And from where I stood
The sea was lingering at my feet
I dusted the meaningless memories
From my mind
And bent to pick up
My sandles I'd kept aside.

Happily Micky took to his heels
To announce my arrival
To my anxiously waiting
And waving friends
I looked up at the sky
And let out a sigh
Soon crushing
The overwhelming sentiments
I raised my head high
Hiding all my pain and suffering
In the garb of a smile
To face the world.

I'll go to my mother
In time
To fold my form
To feel her warmth
And bury my burdens
In her bosom
And lie there
Until . . .
The peace I seek
Starts seeping through me
And nothing hurts me.

LIFE

Life
I know not
When
Thou and I
Shall part
I know not
When,
Where and how
We shall bid
Goodbye
It's hard to part
When we have been
Good friends
Perhaps
You will miss me
And sorry be
Life,
Do bring
Old times to mind
All the warmth
All the love
And all the tender thoughts
That we shared
And if perchance
We do meet again
Will you rekindle
My love again?

THE SEA OF LIFE

I am drifting
In the Sea of life
Life that has
Only shadows of the past
To hang on
Life whose very soul is lost
And all that was once dear to me.

I am like a shipwreck
Soon to be sent
To the scrapyard
Or is it called the
Deathyard?

And those I love the best
Will heave a sigh of relief
As for me
I shall
I hope
Tread the path
Where there are
No tears, no pain, no regrets
Save
The eternal peace
That is all I ask
Of my Creator.

SOLITUDE

I take my refuge
In solitude
Then I dwell upon my thoughts
I look over my shoulders
At the gone-by past
The bitter sweet memories
Are tapered with
Sad and joyful times
The time
That has gone by swiftly
Leaving me behind
With nothing worthwhile
To claim as my own
Except
For my distorted form
I long for scenes
Where no one ever smiles or weeps
And happily to slumber I'll be gone.

THE NAKED SHOCK

Gitanjali has come
Gitanjali has come
Is the general roar
In the School Corridor
From one friend to another
And to those
She still matters most
Gitanjali ! ! !
Is she Gitanjali ? ?
They stare with a naked shock
But they say not much
For the fear of hurting
Whom they still love as much.

Gitanjali is not unaware
Of her beauty shorn
But swallows the pain
With her pride
And offers her smile
After all . . .
Illness too is
A gift of God
And Gitanjali accepts it
With grace and in good stride.

P^{EACE}

Peace
Why do you elude me?
Why this indifference
It sounds so strange that . . .
. We were friends once
Yes, friends
You and I
And now
You have forsaken me
Like a memory lost.

Come, come
Peace
You cannot fool me
I know when you are around

I feel your presence in my mother
When down the slumber I go
I've noticed you in my father
When I eat my dinner for sure
I saw you gleaming in Bibi's eyes
When I first walked few steps
I saw you glow in Aunty Vipala
When I ate up all that she had

I once saw you even on the brow
Of my Doctor
When he first gave me an out pass

I saw you playing silently
The day I visited my house
I saw you beaming through my Pet's eyes
When I stayed with her the night
I saw you flickering
In the eyes of my brother

When we sat up playing cards
Most of the night

I saw you creep into my room
With the first rays of the Sun
I heard you chirping
On my window-sill
To welcome me home
Peace, come be my friend
Like good old times
Please dont . . .
Elude me any-more.

THE REFLECTION OF AGONY

When sorrow grief
And pain are near
And when you know
You are going to lose
Some one most dear
It's time to reach out
For His hand
For He alone knows
What is right
Trust Him and
Leave all else aside.

He has thousand ways
His love and help to show
Soon you will tread
With steadfast feet
With fears and doubts
Left far behind

You are not alone
In this world so wide
Who is afflicted alone
Raise your eyes
And you will find . . . . .
The reflection of your agony
In many more
Thus it will help you
To bear your loss
And with courage
Face the world
With a smile.

SHED NO BITTER TEARS

Mama,
After you lay me
Down to rest
And bathe me
With your tears
Pray do not
Feel let down
For I am leaving you thus

Shed no bitter tears
Nor say to Him unkind

And when you collect
The remains of me
Pray do-not be
Heavy of heart

Let my ashes
Sift through your fingers
Until they join
Where from they came
And be called
The dust again

Dust I may become
But to you and for you
Your Gitanjali I shall always remain.

SOME OTHER SUMMER

She who holds
My heart strings
She who dwells
In my aching heart
She who soothes
My wretched pain
She who cries
Within her heart
She who has suffered much
She who will suffer most
The pangs of parting
Will strangle her heart
To suffocate her
In her happy hours
She who seems
Blissfully unaware
For she often paints
My dreams so bright
She who will weep
All her life
She who will miss me,
Her child
She is the one I'd like
To plead with most
Pray do not weep
When I am no more
Live live Oh please
Live long
For my brother
Who means to me a lot
Who perhaps
Will suffer even more
But he will keep mum

For fear of hurting you
Dear mom
So for our both sake
And for thine
Do not weep Oh mother mine
When I close my eyes
For I'll be only gone to slumber
To meet you again
Perhaps (If God wills it)
In some other Summer.

N APPEAL

Death
Who are you?
Where do you come from?
Where will you take me?
Is the way long?
Is it too dark?

I do claim to be brave
And yet am afraid
For I know not
What's beyond.

Death
I do some times
Expect you
And at times hope
You'd never come
If you must take me
Do be merciful
Take me where no one can hurt me
Or cause me pain
And I have an appeal
Do please be kind
And let me sleep . . .
As in my childhood I did.

THE MOMENT OF TRUTH

Gitanjali is dead
Gitanjali is dead
People are whispering around
A horror of shock
But the moment of truth
That's all
It's all about.

Foolish are those
Who shed tears
Mingled with sorrow and pain
Little do they realise
The joy that is mine
Free of torture
Free of pain
And free of guilt
That shook my faith.

I am now at the thresh-hold
Of my life to start afresh
A new lease of life . . .

The time stands still
The eternity has passed
Gitanjali the child has passed
The mother looks down
Upon the much loved
Blood drained face
Tears trickling down her face
Go my love, go my child
She sighs

I'll be sad
I'll be lonely
I'll be miserable without you
But I'm glad and thankful
To Him the merciful that . . .
At last you my child are at rest.

TEAR DROPS

Two tiny
Tear drops
Weighing heavily
In my eyes
Afraid to shed their burden
For who knows
It might
Pierce the hearts
Of those who care
And burden them ever-more
Their wounded hearts
With shattered hopes
Who attempt in vain
To keep an iron hold.

I meet their eyes
With a surging tide
And marvel at their
Strength and courage
To keep vigil day and night
To watch over me
Lest
I bypass them
While . . .
They are blissfully unaware.

THE WOUNDED BIRD

I am like a wounded bird
Perched upon a bough
My fate is hanging
As if on broken twig

I flutter and fret
Like a bird
In its maiden flight
But I fall back helplessly
'cause I am paralized

I view the world
That passes me by
With moisture in my eyes
It's far beyond measure
What turmoil I feel in-side

When the sun sinks
My heart sinks too
And a sinister feeling
Creeps up
In a cloak of darkness
And stays with me until . . . .

The sifted Sunrays
Embrace me
With their warmth
And make me feel alive

My heart sings
Glory to you Oh God
For granting me
Yet another day . . . .
To be with my Loved Ones.

THE BITTER TRUTH

If I didn't have faith
In thee dear God
The roots of trust
Wouldn't be so deep
As they are.

But the bitter truth
Has stung my very soul
My heart bleeds inwardly
Trying to hide it's
Grief and sorrow
My faith sinks fainting
But fighting ever more
I wonder if anyone can reach
The depth of my woes
The anguish and the life's trials
Have crushed my heart
Within my soul.

I therefore, of my own sweet will
Leave the dusty
Road to others
And keep my soul
Spotless and free
And thus cease . . . . .
The bitter murmur
of Gitanjali's woes.

HAPPINESS

Happiness
I have long stopped
Searching for you
Once you were where I was
And now
You are out of my reach
Pray tell me
What have I done to deserve this

If and when
You do breeze-in
Although its just for a while
I feel the surging tide
Through the windows
Of my eyes
Because I know
You are only paying a short visit
And will be gone in no time

Happiness
I do miss you
I miss you all the time
Next time
You decide to be generous
Please stay a little longer
At least for old times sake
And if you and I must part company
Then please do not return . . . . .
To wake up my sleeping dreams.

IN THE TEMPLE OF MY HEART

The moon light
That shines
In a little puddle
On the rocks

Gradually though
The moon light
Will spread all around
But, right this moment
The little puddle
Reminds me
Of the lamp
That burns
In the temple of my heart.

The glow has been steady
Though I've bourn
Many storms.

The coldness
Is about to envelop me
And my whole being
But, I am not afraid
For I know for sure
No matter how long
Or dark the passage
This little lamp within me
Will burn itself to ashes
In order to guide me
To my destination.

I SMILE IN PAIN

His eyes were sad
When they fell upon me

His voice was
Low and tired

I stared up in wonder
From my day dreaming head
For he seemed
So much unlike him

His eyes had wept
I could tell at a glance

He stood silent
At the foot of my bed
Not once daring
To meet my eyes

He bent his head
And let out a sigh
And held up my hand
He kissed me long
And tenderly
I felt as if
A flame was burning
Inside him.

He is running out
On his bed-side stories
The words die out
On his tongue

He little knows
That I know it all
And wish I could
Do something to help him.
I smile in pain
And do my best
To make his heart
Feel at rest.

DEEP WAVES OF SORROW

In the core
Of my heart
Deep waves
Of sorrow
Flow.

I try my best
To hide
My feelings
But
Sometimes
They overflow.

My hopes
Glisten
No more.
With
Bright thoughts
For the morrow.
They mock at
The sadness
And chide with
My weary heart.

The aching void
Within my soul
Whispers to me
Calmly
Peace be upon you
Gitanjali.

GLIMPSES OF TRUTH

When the sun sets
With it appear
The shadows of the night.

Along comes
The darkness
And then . . .
The stars appear bright.

Grief brings
Glimpes of truth
And reality.

Each sorrow
Takes us few steps
Nearer
The Promised Land of Destiny.

There is no failure
On this road
People can let you down
He will not.

FORGIVE ME

Forgive me
Oh Mother dear
If I go to sleep
And take the
Much needed rest.

I know
You will keep sitting
Beside me and
Watch me until I stir.

I whom thou hast made
With thine own
Flesh and blood
And bore such suffering
To bring me safely
Into this world.

I wish I could pay back
For all that you have done
Not just your duty
But much more.

I wish I could
Reach out to you
And tell you
All that I feel
But I am helpless
Mother
I'll only make you weep.

Need I tell you
How much you mean to me
Whenever you found me

In my slumber
With my lashes studded with tears
You did kiss them away gently
And yet I felt
Warm tears rolling down afresh
You perhaps left your own tears
Behind
By mistake
But I do admit and confess
Your tears brought me
The much needed comfort.

As the day gently enters
Into the softness
Of the night .
I look upon the moon
With moisture in my eyes
Strangely the moon looks
So much like you
And as I painfully close
The shutters of my eyes
You slide back into
The depths of
Those tear filled eyes.

The unshed tears
Weigh heavily
On drug swollen eyes
With pain behind them
Keeping them
From falling
To save you from
More suffering.

There is another version of this poem, almost the same but ending
with the line, *The much needed comfort.*

JUST FOR THIS LOVE

There are times
I feel as though
I am in the
Very gates of hell
Utterly miserable
And past tears.

There are times
I feel absolutely
Numb within.

I wish my heart
Could freeze too
And grow numb
But it doesn't
It remains sensitive
To hurt.

And sometimes
When I am asked something
Such is the constriction
In my throat
That I cannot even
Trust myself to answer.

And yet
Peace and contentment
Start to steal into me
Because inspite of my
Many shortcomings
That I have
It's a beautiful feeling
That . . .
I am loved.

And if
For nothing else
Just for this love
I will endure
My suffering and pain
And will keep still
And wait like the night
With its head bent low
With patience.
The morning will surely come
Come it will
Breaking the sadness
And the emptiness
To replace with smiles.

KARMA

God is not unjust
Nor is He unkind
It's the "karma"
That follows
Soft footed behind
And whether it is right or wrong
He does not wait
For the time
No prayers will help
No love shall hold
And no one can deny
That . . .
The past deeds
Do overtake a man
No matter where
And what time
Hence
Do all good
Say all good
And be kind
It's our deeds
That make our destiny
No, Oh no, God is never unkind.

DREAMS OF A DYING HEART

Beneath the heavy
Load of pain
Beneath the emotional
Stress and strain
Beneath the ache
Lies a heart
Inside this heart
Lie the dreams . . .
. . .the dreams . . .
Of a dying heart
Dreams of a . . .
Budding flower.

The dreams
Crying out in vain
To reach the sky
And pluck the stars.

The dreams
That unfold
Untold joy
My dreams are
One could never dream of
And I dream of these
Impossible dreams
I wonder if my dreams
Will ever come true
And if I will survive
To see them bloom.

DEAR GOD

Dear God:
Please hear my prayer
Give me the strength
To accept your will
And forgive me for
My sins if any.
If you think it fit
To take me
Then please give
Strength and courage
To those who love me
And help me
Not to rail in self-pity.
Asking why?
But to have faith
And to know that . . .
Your will is best
Help me!
Oh, please help me
To trust you
Not from fear but
Because of Love and Faith.

ROSARY

Watching beside my bed
In the dark and silent night
Your fingers keep moving
Over the string of beads
Praying for my life
I'm not asleep
Though you think I am
I too am praying
Only I have no Rosary
My helpless hands are tied up
With tubes and needles
But like you
I am also waiting
For the faint gleam
That will dispell
The night's cold gloom
Until the sunlight
Steals into my room and
The shadows and doubts
Clear away
Then my heart will murmur
Thank you God
For sending me yet
Another day.

ENDURANCE

The Spring is here
And the rod like bough
Is studded with budding flowers

A swift response
Of sympathy
Wells up within my heart
I can no longer bear
This constant endless aggravating pain
Oh please God
Let me not be swept off
In the torrents of selfpity

Like thunder clouds
About to break
I have exhausted
My store of endurance

Before my faith too fails me
And I go insane
Please God have mercy upon me
And take me away.

ON THE SEASHORE OF LIFE

On the sea shore
I often go
to watch the waves
come and go,
The waves wash
the pebbles bright:
I pick them up, in turn,
to find
the one
which I like the most.
Joyfully I bring it home.
We, too, are like these pebbles
On the sea shore of life
And when God wants
He takes us away.
Whether it is day or night,
whenever we feel proud
of our possessions,
He comes.
Why deny God His choice?

THE PAST AND THE PRESENT

With past and present
in view,
I weigh the joys and
the sorrows . . .
in cue.
And when I think of
His kindness to me,
in the years
gone by,
my head hangs
in shame
indeed
for asking Him:
Why? God, why?

I have at length
accepted His Will
and resigned to
my fate.
I have given Him
all my trust and faith.

UNTIL THE SUNSET HOUR

It is very early
The sky is still grey
With shadows of the night
And yet
I feel as if
Everything is bathed
In Sunshine.

Indeed I feel dazzled
With the brilliance
Of my own joy
When a little while later
The sun did break through
It seemed somehow dim
In comparison
With my own emotions
I am going "Home" today
There was one particular
Bright star
Which seemed
A little nearer the earth
And yet
How far away
As far as hope from my life
But I'm happy
Though
My heart is weary
I hope my happiness will last
Until
The Sunset hour.

I TRUST YOU STILL

I trust you
Still
Oh my dear dear God
Though the sorrows
Keep falling
Like the rain drops.

I trust Thee
Yet
Though You have
Betrayed my trust
And refused me
All that I yearn for.

The Xmas is here
There is music
In the air
I have but
Sweet old memories
Tapered with love and care
Which I now unfold
With great pain and
Much sorrow.

Cry I will never
Weep I will not
I left these stupid
Emotions behind me
For a long time now.

This mighty
Unknown
Sea of death
Does pass a shudder
Through me I confess
I sway at the thought of it
But dear God
Your nearness holds me
In a grip.
Isn't it amazing
For I trust you
Still.

THE BEAUTIFUL TREE

As I lay
sick in bed
slipping and sinking
into the webs of death

I watched
the much loved rain
and was amazed
at the anger
of the wind that blew
it whistled
and set my scarf to and fro.

Next morning
when all was quiet and calm
I looked out of the window
and something was gone

The rain last night
tore the top of the beautiful tree
the only soothing sight
for my fast dimming eyes

My feeble heart nearly broke
when I saw the splendour
of my much loved flowers
scattered around
on the wet grass.

HELP ME DEAR GOD

As I sit in my solitude
And walk my lonely path
Suddenly
I feel your hand in mine
And I feel warm and secure
You never leave my side
Even though I stumble . . .
Your love picks me up
And gives me strength
To face each new day
And courage to overcome
Anguish and pain.

Help me dear God
To keep myself clean and pure
In thought, word and deed
Help me to be merciful
To those who hurt me
And to those who need me
Help me to spread
Whatever little happiness I can
Whether it be by word
A smile or a touch of hand.

Oh God, help me to rest tonight
Beneath the protection
And the warmth of your love
And let me arise tomorrow
To give thanks to you
For a peaceful night.

PROMISE

Promises are made
To break
I've neither learn't
Nor was told
Promise is a . . .
Beautiful thing
I have known
One can live on a promise
And die for
When
Once made
Promise is never made
In a hurry nor in vain
Promise can sometimes
Help the person
To retain
The hope and the strength
And to defy
The call of death
Promise is not made
Just for the moment
Promise is for a lifetime to share
I too am living
On one such promise
Once made to me
In sure earnestness
And I shall wait
Hoping
That this promise will not break
Or else
Not just the promise
But
I will break.

LIFE THE SLIPPING SAND

I am drowned
In the midst
Of my thoughts
Thoughts that . . .
Weigh me down
To the lowest ebb
Thoughts that are woven
Like a spider's web
Stretching their pattern
Intricate enough to hold me
In the grip of fear
Yea, fear
Fear of death, fear of beyond
And fear of the unknown.

Alas! life is like the slipping sand
I see it go at the end of each day
Far away in the distance
The Sun is lying low
With all it's glory behind him
It makes me feel sad to let him go
As slow, yet as swiftly
As my life goes
From day to day.

I sit back with sadness
Weighing heavily on my mind
Only with thoughts all around me
Taking me down the memory lane
To remind me all that was once mine
The joy of love, the gift of life
Good health and the blessings of dear ones
And above all
Being blessed by God

With parents such as mine
Who share with me
My joy and sorrow
And bear the pain
Not just in heart
But in tears-divine
Their healing touch
Is like the balm that soothes
And their smiles light up my dreary nights.

The flowers that stand
Alongside my bed
Beautiful, proud and adorable
In time they too will be dead
Just as I will be
And discarded like waste
That's life, isn't it?
Praise to you Oh God
Why should I be sad
If flowers can die
Who are so young and lovely to behold
So beautiful and so pure
Then, who am I?

THE HEART OF GOLD

Grannies are many
And many more there will be
But this Granny
I am talking about
Is none other than
My Bibi.

My Granny is not
Just mine
(Though very much she's my own)
She's in no small measures too
Yes, that's exactly what she is
With a heart of gold and as large
As the ocean wide.

Sympathetic she is to the core
She'll deny herself a morsel
And feed you more
She is always there when needed
Sunshine, rain or thunder
Whether it will cost her health
She little cares for that
Just that moment all she cares
Is that you need her care.

If I am not much in pain
It's because . . .
She's on war-path with HIM
Her prayers go hand-in-hand
With my Grandpa's
Knock the doors of
Heaven above
And melt the heart of God.

I worship the ground
She walks on, and kiss her
With my eyes — bless her soul!
She is the most adorable
'Cause, she's not just my Grandma
She's the maker of my mother divine.

When she laughs
I like her best
For she has those moments rare
I pray to God and wish her well
For all times to come
May God give her
Tons of courage
To cover my form
With a touch-of-iron
In her heart of gold.

THE SOUND OF SILENCE

The sound of silence
is over-bearing
my feeble heart
and soul.
It's knawing at me,
day and night, even
when people around
me are galore.

The sound of silence
is deffening for I am
carried away by my thoughts
even though when it's a
pin-drop silence
my mind is in chaos.

There are so many
questions I ask myself
but meet a sound-proof wall
the same sound . . .
of silence
bounces back
and hits me hard.

This sound of silence
will soon one day
carry me to the . . .
Silent Tower
which I often see
in my dreams . . .
upon the hill-top.

The way to the tower
is well trodden
hence
I am not afraid to go
for I have not sinned
or wronged any living soul.

THE BIRTHDAY GIFT

Hanging in my wardrobe
is a dress, dream come true.
It's just the thing I wanted
all these years through.

It's a dress bought
with tons of love
from many many miles,
it's not the money
which went in it but
the joy, the pleasure
and the smiles.

I wore it for a short while,
touching it with love and care,
but soon hung it back in cupboard
for I didn't want to be tempted
to wear. 'cause it's my . . .
"Birthday Gift", which is just a . . .
few months away.

But I do often want to see it
and make sure it's there.
For it's not really just a dress
it's a whole lot more. The love,
the care, the sentiments, and
the devotion all speak through it.
Just to say . . .
"HAPPY BIRTHDAY TO YOU".

Gitanjali never did wear her "Birthday Dress". For just before she was to dress for her "Birthday Party" she collapsed and was driven away in an ambulance, never to return home again.

THE HARP

I am being used
by God like a
harp.
One moment
He caresses me
like a fond child,
next minute
He grasps me firmly
and strikes.

A sharp quick blow
that wrings me with
pain,
torturing me by
pulling at my
heart-strings
in vain.
And just when I am
about to snap,
He rests my head
with warmth on His chest.
Softly and tenderly
He holds me to His heart
and wipes away my tears
to replace them with . . .
laughs.

THE JOURNEY OF LIFE

When too much of sun
Withers the flowers
Then the nature takes its course

The rain comes bouncing
Hither and Thither
And every-thing is in chaos

The sun takes shelter
Behind the clouds
While the clouds hang
Frightingly thick and black
But fear not my frail soul

For this is the journey of life.

The joy the sorrow
The cry the laughter
Each follows like
Day follows the night
Dont lose your heart
Stay firm and take
Every-thing in good stride

The sky will clear
The sun will shine
The trees will look bathed
The birds will chirp happily
And so will your heart
And the rainbow will appear bright.

Pain and sorrow
Tears and smiles
The ups and downs
Remember
If there was no contrast
You would never appreciate
The good things of life.

I HEARD A BIRD SINGING

All of a sudden
it rained last night.
I heard a bird
singing outside.

How I wish
I could understand
your language, my friend.

The night had
a nip in the air:
you, perhaps, lacked
the warmth in your nest,
and were singing to call
your mate, for help.

I thought of you
long after
your singing ceased,
wondering . . .
whether it was
a joyful song, or
were you singing
about your grief.

I have, however,
learnt a lesson
from you, my friend:
why should I stop singing
just because I am unwell.

Maybe the song
calms the storm
and helps to disperse
my doubts and fears,
leaving room only
for cheer.

FAREWELL MY FRIENDS

It was beautiful
As long as it lasted
The journey of my life.

I have no regrets
Whatsoever save
The pain I'll leave behind.

Those dear hearts
Who love and care
And the heavy with sleep
Ever moist eyes
The smile inspite of a
Lump in the throat
And the strings pulling
At the heart and soul.

The strong arms
That held me up
When my own strength
Let me down
Each morsel that I was
Fed with was full of love divine.

At every turning of my life
I came across
Good friends
Friends who stood by me
Even when the time raced me by.

Farewell
Farewell
My friends

I smile and
Bid you goodbye
No, shed no tears
For I need them not
All I need is your smile.

If you feel sad
Do think of me
For that's what I'll like
When you live in the hearts
Of those you love
Remember then . . .
You never die.

REMEMBER...

Remember...
The night your eyes
Were fighting sleep,
And
I, my fate.
Remember...
The rain kept pouring
Like the tears from your eyes,
And
Thunder too was laughing aloud.
As if, mocking at my sinking life.

I hardly could breathe.
Yet, I managed a prayer.

I said to God, "Just this one time please ! ! "
Spare my Mother, the ordeal.
She is very tired and
Is falling to sleep.
Be merciful God, let her
Rest for the night.

My prayer, indeed was granted.
For I soon saw you were asleep.

I saw your profile
From the corner of
My tear-dripping eyes.
You sat cuddled on a chair.
With your feet and knees
Tucked-in,
Your back reclining

Against a grey wall.
Even though pathetic,
You made a pretty picture.
Your weary head cradled,
In the nook of your arm.

My heart went out to you Mother,
On that rainy night.

How I wished, I could just then
Be by your side.
Touch you, ever so gently, and
Put all your fears aside. But,
I could do not thus, and lay
Just as helpless.
With only longing tugging
At my heart-strings.

I promise you Mother,
I'll fight my fate.
Until . . .
If only, I could see you smile,
Just once! minus,
The pain in your eyes.

A PEACEFUL NIGHT

As the day gently
Enters into the
Softness of the night
I painfully raise
My drug sodden eyes
To catch a glimpse
Of the lamp that hangs
From the clear sky.

Strangely
The moon soothes
My aching heart
And the memories
Of childhood
Come gushing along

The notes of a familiar song
Plays on my mind.

I smile when I remember
The silly things
We some-times
Said or did
Only to cheer me up
And happily put me to sleep.

I now recall those memories
With moisture in my eyes
And send up a fervent prayer
Oh! God please give me
A peaceful night.

WOUNDED PRIDE

Tender is the age.
Tender are the thoughts
and if someone treads on them
It will only break my heart.

Before the dreams can
wake and scream
for the freedom of thought,
the pain entwines itself
around my wakeful hours.

Youth, beauty and
innocence:
all three, hand-in-hand,
feel crushed . . .
against their fate and
their wounded pride.

MERCY OH GOD

Before
I request you
For your mercy
Oh, God please
Hear my prayer

Help all those
Who like me are ill
And cannot sleep for pain.

Help all those
Who are poor and friendless.
Help all those
Who are sad and lonely.

Bless all those
I love and care.

And please God
Have mercy upon me.
Help me, oh, please
Help me to sleep
Just for awhile.

And forgive me
If I am . . .
Being too demanding.

THE BREATHLESS STORM

The breathless storm
Which has gathered
Darkly around me
Is gradually going
To gather me like dust.

Afraid though I am
Of the storm
But yet . . .
I trust Him.

When darkness veils
My wounded soul,
I try not to sink
Into the depths
Of my woes.

I have wept until
I can weep no more
I prayed and still pray.
My faith is all that
Clings to me
While all else is lost.

Yes, it does confuse me
No doubt:
But then He alone knows
What is best.

MY DADDY

I'll let you into a secret
There's a kind soul I know
Who dwells in my heart
From the time unknown
It's from him that I gain
My strength, courage and hope
He keeps kindling my heart
With each cherished glance
It's fuel of his love that
Makes my heart glow

He sits up beside me
With my head cradled in his arms
He tells me lovely tales
And warms up my shattered heart
He takes my cares away
And soothes my aching heart

His heart bleeds within his soul
He tries his best to act
But he little knows about
His Bul-bul
That she chirps
Only
To make him feel swell.

Published in *Eve's Weekly*, Feb. 10 16, 1979

AT THE HOUR OF DEATH

At the hour
Of
Death
The time
Hangs heavily
Pulling at the
Heart strings
That are already
Worn and torn
With emotional
Stress and strain.

The load
Of sorrow
Is so painful to bear
And yet
We hold back
The flood gates
Of unshed tears
That edge along
To gush out
Their pent up
Frustrations.

Helpless
To keep
At bay
The hour set
By the unseen
Hand of Destiny
And in silence
We bow down
To accept His Will.

NO MORE TEARS TO SHED

Have you seen
A soul in sadness
Who bears her pain and sufferings
With a smile
If not
Come peep into my eyes
And you will have
The glimpse of that sight.

Have you ever heard
The sound of a brave
But
A breaking heart
Come hold me then
A little closer to thine heart.

Have you ever seen
The pain of sorrow
It reflects
Through the eyes of those
Who love and care
And die every moment
With my each falling sigh.

There are bruised hearts
Which are torn within
But bear it up with a smile
With songs on their lips
To cheer me up
And sit all night
By my side.

The warmth
Of their healing touch
The eyes brimming
With love and tears
Which cannot be held for long
Mine own tears
Have made
A permanent track
Like a short-cut through the lawn.

But now
I have no more tears to shed
Nor the desire to fight
I have taken my leave
From the world
And accepted
Gods will in good stride.

Have you ever heard
My haunting voice
In the deep silence
Of the night
Of sending up tender
Heartfelt prayers
To the Almighty God above
To bless those
I leave behind
Who have been
So good and kind.

THE SILENT SIREN

We have lived and loved
Through sunshine and
Through cloudy weather.
We have shared
Each others joys
And cried each others
Tears.
We have smiled together
To soothe away
The vexed moments
Of our life and
Laughed at silly things
To make life bearable and
Bright.

Remember . . .
The times we clung together
When the siren would sound
In the days of the war?
Remember how I held on to you
Thinking it was the end of the world

Now when my own end is in sight
I've strangely grown wiser
But, alas!
This is no false alarm
And I am alone shattered
By this silent siren
Of my death sentence.

When the clouds of sorrow
Lowered upon me
And you stopped meeting

My eyes
I cried and cried
My heart out but
Only in the night.

No matter whatever happens
No matter what-may-come
I'll gladly share
My joys with you
But, the tears . . .
Are all mine.

RESPITE

Be silent
Oh please be silent
Let me hear
The whisper of God

He cares
Oh he does care

For he has
Answered my prayers

All my troubles
Are melting away
And my pain with-held

I am happy
Oh I am really happy
As I've never been before

I am feeling
At my best
With my family
Home and my pets

If perchance
You cared to whisk me away
I shall have no regrets
For you have shown
Consideration, love and care
And gave me
The much needed . . .
Respite.

THE WINDOW-PANE

Whenever I feel
weary or depressed
or I'm in pain.
I just sit by myself
and look out through
the window-pane.

The sky looks
unblemished,
just like my soul.
Yet, at times, it's
spotted with dark
clouds of envy that
float in me, for the
birds that soar.

Here, I lie, helplessly
tied to my bed,
awaiting . . .
the death sentence!
neither caring nor daring
to welcome my guest.

ALL I DESIRE

When you caress me
Fondly
And kiss me
With thine eyes.
I'm afraid
I may breakdown
And
Drown you
In the tide.

Every moment
Of
My life
I know not
What may happen
Next.
All I desire
And want is
You should be there
When
I meet . . .
My end.

I AWAIT YOU

There's a strange kind
of suffocation.
Stranger still is
the reason.
That I await you,
with much longing,
mixed feelings.

Whether you will
return
or turn your back
on me for good,
I do not know.
And yet,
I await you.

OSCAR

On my window-sill
I threw some crumbs
Hoping and waiting
That Oscar might come.

The other birds
Flew-in
To peck
But the one I waited most
Did not turn up
In the end.
I gave up waiting
And wondered where he goes . . .
To beg for breakfast,
And mend his soul.

My little visitor
Is a crow called
'Oscar'.
Surprised?
I am sure you are,
So was I, when I first
Discovered
Oscar was a friend
Of my friend.

Dear Mrs. Flo Gubbay,
My heart weeps
When I recall
How difficult it was
To bid you goodbye.
But then, who was I

To tell you . . .
Please dont go!!
Not just I but
All the birds, all
The animals in the
Entire neighborhood
Are going to miss you
For sure.

You have been their
God-Mother and the one
Who really cared.
They will long for you
And so will I
And remember you until . . .
The end of time.
Oh! dear Mrs. Gubbay
You are divine.

Oscar's one leg was broken, and used to limp. After Mrs. Gubbay left for New York he started visiting Gitanjali. Each morning Oscar would come and share the breakfast with her. When Gita fell ill and was in the hospital Oscar did come but having no one to feed him he drifted away. He did however come back to pay us a visit. Gita in her state of paralysis would request her Daddy to take her near the window so that she could see her friend and feed him.

DO NOT WEEP MY FRIENDS

When I am lying mutely
Wrapped in the garb of white
Pray do not weep my friends
And thus bid me goodbye.

Do not weep my friends
When I am laid down to rest
For the last and final journey
And pray do not lay wreaths
Wet with tears
Do please join in the prayers
For that's all I need
To bring solace to my soul.

I would like you
To fold your hands
And thank God
For His mercy
Aren't you glad
Someone you loved
Is free of pain at last?

Every heart has it's sorrows
Every heart has it's pain
But if you lose your courage now
All will be in vain.

We all have our share
Just as the Earth needs
Sunshine and rain
So does our soul need
The joy, the sorrow, and the pain.

The remains of my dust
Will flow freely
In the river-bed
And if you look up
You will find
The rainbow of...
Tears that I shed.

Published in *Mirror*, Aug. 1979

96

THE BEACON

The hope
That wavers
Day by day
The dreams
That keep
Slipping away
The desire
To live
Is burning bright
Appealing with God
Day and night
I ponder
But try not to think
Too deep
For then
My heart seeps in tears
Leaving room only for fear
And that's the one-thing
I abhore most.

Therefore
With a trust
Most rare
I am following
The beacon
Thou has set
Leaving my life's boat
For you to steer
And reach me
Where you wish and care.

THE FRAGILE THREAD

Life is like a
Fragile thread
One does not know
When it might snap

The only solid
Hold on it
Is the faith
That is . . .
If
You trust and care

Be prepared
To face death
As and when
She appears
Death is like a
Honoured guest
She comes not
On her own
She has His orders
To abide.

Do not be afraid
Death is all warm
Soft and kind . . .
To all those
Who trust
His Judgement.

MISTY EYES

My misty eyes
Are growing hazier
But the hope is
Flickering yet

My end is near
I sure know
But there is undying
Urge to live once more

To walk again
On the dew kissed grass
And run to aid
The sightless man

To walk a while
With lonesome heart
And help to write
A note of love

To pluck a flower
And place it in the hands
I most adore
To hug my mother
Close to me
With a longing She'd never know
With hands free of
Tubes and needles

To shake her hand
With my friends
With strength

To show my gratitude
To run my dogs
For a mile and
Replace their smiles
They look upon me
So dolefully sad
It breaks my heart
For they understand
Strange but true
These dumb friends
Are better than many
Human beings
Who say they love
And care yet never
Burn the fuel of
Their love to help
You from the cold
That awaits to
Envelop you.

GOOD WISHES

Happy birthday
Happy birthday
Many cards and
Greetings I get.

Down the dark
Passage of life
I travel with
The good wishes
Of you my dear
Friends.

My pathway
Lights up
With lightning
That thunder strikes.

Your good wishes
Stand by me,
Even though
My future stands
Shaky
Day and night.

THE WITHERED FLOWERS

The bright hopes
I once dreamt
Are now blurred
And left far behind

The human ties
That bind me
Will too be broken
In time.

Any trace of me
Even if you seek
You shall never find
Except perhaps on
These pages left behind
And if you care to look
You will find . . .
The fragrance of
The withered flowers
Which too
To me you denied.

I see your future
In the distance when
Your heart will feel
Weary and restless
The sleep too will
Elude you and
Find you in distress.

The tears that will roll
Unguarded and catch you unaware
Your heart will then
Swell up and choke you
For not having kept
Your promise.

102

I WONDER

Do you know
My days are numbered
And I have so much of
Task at hand

To feed the down
And poor
And wipe their tears
With my hands
To see them happy
Cheerful and help them
Whatever I can.

Do you know
My days are numbered
And I have so many
Dreams yes, so many
Dreams to make them
Come true
For which I have
Miles to tread
And I have
No strength left.

Would He grant me
Sufficient time
To achieve my goal
I wonder?
And to enjoy
The rest of my days
Even though . . .
They are numbered.

MEMORIES DEAR AND SAD

The thoughts of you
Weighing heavily on my mind
Stacked up with
Memories dear and sad.

I feel the storm
Within my breast
Oh, please come soon
Before . . .
I forever rest.

All I seek
Is a little glance
Of love
And the healing touch
Of your hand.

The hand that held me as a little babe
The hand that rocked my cradle away
The hand that made me feel secure
The hand that taught me first to write
The hand that looped my curls away
The hand that threw me up in the air
Only to grasp me back with care
The hand that wiped my tears away
The hand that tucked me safely in bed.

I longed for that hand
Then and long for it now
But wonder why
I'm being denied
Just when I need
That hand most
More than you would ever know.

I ask for no riches
I ask for no worldly gifts
I ask for nothing
In return of my love
Except for . . .
The warmth of that hand
So that
I may die in peace
Knowing that you did
Love and care
And came to see me
At . . .
My death bed.

BE STRONG MY SOUL

Be strong my soul
Though
Death looms in view
Be strong my soul
Do not grieve or brood
Be strong my soul
For there is much to bear
For you my dear
And for all those who care
The pangs of parting
Are most difficult I bet
Yet,
Be bold my soul
And stoop not low
By begging for mercy
And prayers galore
For then you will embarrass God
In His own sweet Home.

Be strong my soul
Do not rail in self-pity
Let Him torture or
Sow the ground with thorns
Keep your chin up
With all your heart
Be strong my soul
Death may be kind
Do not judge her so harshly
Maybe it's not the right time
But He knows best
For He has not failed thee yet.

Only I plead with you
Dear God
To be granted . . .
A little time
To be given the privilege
Of the 'Gold Thread' tying
Let my love shine
Upon it's way
Today, tomorrow
And all the way
Only Winks will know
The mighty grief
If you are not kind
So do please, Dear God, be kind
For then there will be peace
That comes after the sorrow
A peace there will be
In a life subdued
But will heave a sigh
Though inlaid with sadness and tears.

DON'T BE SO LATE

I know not
How long I have to wait
Before you decide
To keep the promise you made
To return to my longing arms
Arms that may raise no more
To welcome you
Because they are dying
For lack of strength.

The feeling of isolation
And loneliness which I felt
When I last kissed you goodbye
Has swept over me afresh
I tremble at the thought
Of not seeing you again
Don't be so late
To visit me my Papa dear!
For raise me you will never
From the Dust!

Even passers-by
Stop by me
To offer me their sympathies
Tears and smiles
In silence they seem to ask me
What I wish or desire
I cast my eyes downwards
And reply them not.

Death is just at the corner
Waiting to sting me
While my gaze is hazy
And fading ever more
The hope is still flickering
To see you
Walk through the door.

When many people
Will throng the way
On the way
To my last journey
Silently shedding tears in pity
Showering me with profound love
And flowers
I wonder if you will be
Amongst them
Silently walking behind me
Or resting my coffin on your shoulders
Where once you carried me
To give me a joy-ride
When I was a child.

I PRAY TODAY

I pray today
in all earnestness
with all my heart and soul
for those whose hands
have reared me
and held me close
for those who have caressed
and ceased my pain
and borne the suffering with me;
for those whose hearts
have wept in grief
and yet
sung happy songs to me;
for those who show
the patience rare
and help me
to keep my cool;
for those who dwell
in my bruised heart
and keep me wrapped
with the warmth of their love.
How can any harm
come to me,
when I am protected
with an armour of love.

Published in BEAUTIFUL, Sept. 1979

110

ENCHANTING MEMORIES

Shimmering on the rocks
like a whirlpool studded
with diamonds, is the sea
just below my house —
called, the Dolphin.

This is where first grew
the roots of my childhood
dreams . . .
dreams that I started to
knit, with much love and
care.
Stealing the hues from
the glorious flowers,
the rainbow and the sunset.

I got carried away . . .
with the tide of time,
forgetting, life has its
share of ups and downs.

Today for instance . . .
I'm fully awake,
from my day-dreaming head.
Shattered and shaken
with a rude shock!
my childhood strangely
somewhere lost.

In pensive mood,
in shades of blue and
positive pain which

tears me through.
I stand sadly apart,
to view my past.
No, I have no regrets,
when I think of my share
of happiness.

I cling to my
enchanting memories,
steadfast. And
thank the Lord for
the sound of music
and the roar of the sea below,
which lulls me and takes me back
to times . . .
that are no more.

MY BROTHER

I have a big brother
But he is only big
In name.
I am the one
Who bullics him
And
Makes him cry in vain.

I love and adore him
And bore him no end
With the games of Chinese-checkers
And cheating immense.

He is crazy about many things
Including jeans and stickers
You'll find one
On his knee-cap
And
Another under his bum.

He is a bit crazy.
Not in the sense
You guess:
It's music
He's mad about
And there's nothing
That can be done.

He is a book-worm
And
Loves to stamp his name
Whether it's on his book
Or mine
He cares a damn.

He loves me better
Than
He ever did before
May be he feels
Sorry for me but
Doesn't like to show it.

I love him better too
I confess
Than I ever did before
But in my case it's different:
Then I was only a child
Which I am not anymore.

MOTI MY FRIEND

Moti my friend,
I miss you no end.
I think of you
Each time, I see
The loaf of bread.
I can only request
People to see
If you are being
Fed.

I care for you
In a very special way
Which you'd never know
Anyway.

I think of you
When I am snug
And kept warm.
Wondering . . .
If you are shivering
With lack of love
Or has someone
Pitied you
And given you
A rug.

Each morning when
I am driven to hospital
The glimpse of you
And your faithful paw
Which you hand me
Through the window

Of the car.
My heart whispers
A prayer for you
May you find a friend
To take care of you.

Moti was a stray dog, born on the roadside. Gitanjali, her friends and Mrs. Gubbay had named him Moti. He was known as the building-dog. Mrs. Gubbay had gone to the extent of registering his name and putting a collar around Moti's neck, with his name and the licence number. Once Mrs. Gubbay had left for the States, and Gita for hospital, Moti had no one place to go to beg for food. The servants sometimes did care but not for long. Moti's collar had been removed by miscreants. Moti has not been seen around for long.

TREAD SOFTLY OH FRIEND

Tread softly
Oh friend
My dreams
Are
Scattered around.
Crush them not
Under thy feet
Nor
Consider them
Not.
I still dream
The promise of
Joyfilled tomorrows.
Tomorrows,
That may or
May not
Cross my path
And yet,
I dream.
Although
My dreams
Are
Scattered around
Therefore
My friend
Tread softly,
Crush not my dreams
For they are
Too feeble to protest.

THE TIME IS RUNNING OUT

My life is
Like a tide
One minute
The hope
Rises
The next minute
It's low.
Who knows
Who can tell
When it might
Finally be
No more.

Please unlock
The gates of your
Heart
And let my love
Flow in.
I may warm and
Perhaps
Change your heart
For me.

You'll not be
Any poorer
If you at least
Write to me
My eyes
Long to see
The words
Which you haven't
Uttered to me.

Just once,
Oh! please,
Just once
Show up
Now that . . .
The time is running out.
When will you come
When the clock cannot
Be put back??

THE REWARD OF MY FRIENDSHIP

I wish you were my Daddy
And I your darling child
I wouldn't be thanking you
The way I am thanking you
Tonight.

Ardent fan I was yours
Ardent fan I am now
Thank you my friend
For offering your hand
When
I need it most.

I have seen
Your many moods
Good, bad, and blue
But your eyes could weep
I never knew.

The reward of my friendship
Is the tears that you have shed
The soothing and the healing touch
The warmth in your eyes
Holds a promise for me
Though . . .
Death is in sight.

I am grateful to you
For all that you've done
There's so much to thank
There would be no-end.

Deep in your heart
I am sure you know
Each word I say is
From the bottom of
My soul.

WITH DIGNITY

When you caress me
Fondly and kiss me
With thine eyes
I'm afraid, I may
Break down and
Drown you in the . . .
Tide.

Every moment
Of my life
I know not
What may happen
Next.
All I desire
And want is . . .
You should be there,
When . . .
I meet my end.

When the actual
Time of parting
Nears
Be brave, and
Do not fear.
Just be near me
And hold my hand
With utter Trust
Give in to HIM
And let me too
Die with dignity.

STARS IN MY EYES

Walking through the valley
With dew-kissed grass
Beneath my feet.
The birds chirping upon
The treetops happily.
The cows walking merrily
With the sound of music
Around their neck.
The herd of sheep
Walking closely knitted
Bleating at the intrusion
With protest.
The love of my life
The horses
Grazing in the far off fields.
The solo howl
Of a stray dog
Who has no friend to care
Except his own reflection
He sees in the stagnate water
As he stares.
The crystal clear
Springs on the way
That help us nourish
Our thirst.
The Sunrise
In it's infancy
Raises its head
To greet the world.
Stretching its arms
Full of warmth
To inwrap the world.

Giving much joy and happiness
Just as at the end of each day
The Sun with all its glory
Lowers his tired head to rest.
Bringing about a touch of gloom
As he enfolds his eyes
Suddenly there's a nip in the air.

I too like the Sun
Will sink soon
With stars in my eyes.
Leaving behind the radiance . . .
Of love.
Shining through your eyes.

I LOVE YOU

I love you,
In thousand
Different ways.
I love you
Through n' through
I love you
For your pain you suffer and
For the joy you give.
I love you
For the tiring times
When all you did was
Smile.
I love you
For your lullabys
Though your heart
Wept-inside.
I love you
For your love for animals
And for the sick and poor
I love you
For your cooking,
And for mad things you
Sometimes do. Like;
Remember . . .
The ride-in-the bus?
When the city was wet
The thunder threatened
To tear the sky, and
We both sat snug
Holding-hands.
The wind was strong
So was I, I defied

The wind and put up
The window, you yelled
But, I did not hear.
The rain was on my face
Kissing me tenderly and
Slipping away.
I love you
For your every act,
Except
When you get over-protective
Then I really get ragged
For then, I'm mad at you
And couldn't care if you were hurt.
But, a little later as always
We make-up and giggle.
I love you
For my-cake-baking-sessions
For using away all the butter
Just when you needed it most
You stopped dumb and
Could not even utter . . .
Then a peal of laughter
Broke the awkward silence
While all my friends were around
Then one-by-one
Each of us joined
The beautiful sound of laughter
And licked our buttery-fingers.
It's a boon to have a Mom like you
Who can feel one with all —
Little children or old people
You are loved by them all.

THE DAY OF JUDGEMENT

It was the first dawn
of my awareness of
how short I was of
time.
The impact
of this knowledge
was so painful that
I soon overcame
my feelings of hurt and
placed myself and my trust
in the palm of His hand.
Hence, my friends,
do not feel sorry for me,
for I am above
all that hurts.
And eagerly, though not
yet, I await
the day of judgement.

PEACE BE UPON YOU

In the core
Of my heart
Deep waves
Of sorrow
Flow.

I try my best
To hide
My feelings
But
Sometimes
They overflow.

My hopes
Glisten
No more.
With
Bright thoughts
For the morrow.
They mock at
The sadness
And chide with
My weary heart.

The aching void
Within my soul
Whispers to me
Calmly
Peace be upon you
Gitanjali.

THE GOODBYE

You waved me not
goodbye.
You looked me not
in the eyes.

You merely
retreated
while I held
my breath.

You walked away
into . . .
the wilderness
leaving me thus.
Without
a tear or a sigh.

THE COURTS OF LAW

Strength of character
I have always possessed
Strength to bear pain
Has stayed with me
Hand-in-hand.
But strength to nurse
My wounded heart
I'm often at a loss
To understand and wonder
Wherefrom do I get my strength.
To face each new day and the ordeals
Of the unbearable pain.

Strength too like love
Has it's roots deeply
In-laid
In trust and faith.

My faith lies within my reach
My faith lies in my Daddy
Who to me is like a God
Silently suffering
But speaking not.

Strength is thus born
In deep silence of . . .
Long suffering hearts.

Faith is born in trust
The trust seeps through
My Daddy's clasp.
If his faith does not shake
Nothing can nor will
Eradicate my faith.

My strength thus is the outcome of . . .
My Daddy's unfailing devotion.
He cries when I cry
He licks my tears dry
He suffers as much as I do
His suffering is untold
He suffers for he knows
The hands of destiny
Will soon snatch away
His little Chintu girl.

I am his baby, wont you be
Just, Oh! God.
Dont let the world decide this
In the stone-built-courts-of-law.

I whom he has held
Close to his heart
And gave love in abundance
Unasked.
He has bestowed upon me
The warmth from his burning heart,
And supports me like a rock.
Hoping, wishing, and desiring
To snatch for me the stars.
He laughs with me, when I laugh
But cries behind my back
He has come too close to me
To hide anything he has
My heart goes out to him
When I find him smiling at me
Desperately trying hard to amuse me
By telling me silly things.
I play up to him, to help him to
Cease that painful look that peeps through
The shutters of his eyes, which he tries his
Best to hide.

131

THE APPROACHING STORM

The sea looks
Calm and still.
Yet,
There is thunder
In the star-scattered
Sky.
The moon is somewhere
Nearby
I can tell, from . . .
The silver-lingerie
Around the edges,
Of the clouds.

The lightning
Struck,
A while ago
The thunder again
Roared like a lion.
What kind of storm
Is approaching!
Neither I can tell,
Nor I know,
Why.

The effect of it,
Is disturbing.
'cause all is quiet,
Within my heart.

THE PARTLY OPEN WINDOW

Last night,
The moon
Visited me.
Through,
The partly
Open-window.

He somehow
Looked,
Sad and weary.
And
Soon hid himself
Behind a cloud.
The cloud was
See through,
And I saw it all.

The memories
Of childhood
Came gushing
Along . . .
When,
As a babe,
Mom held me,
On her waist
Pointing
To the moon
To cheer me up.

The tears
Did sparkle
Instead of
Spilling
And
I would smile away
To a dreamy-land.

How I wish
I were a babe
Again
And you moon
Had
The same magic of
The goneby days.

YOUR MESSAGE

My eyes are
glued,
Under the
Door.
Wherefrom
Your message
Will come.

In a feverish
Response,
I'll grab
The letter,
And hold it
Against
My throbbing
Heart.

What you have to
Say,
Is up to you.
What my eyes will
Scan for,
Is up to me.

THE DEPARTURE

When my time comes
For the departure
Reluctantly though
I'll bid you goodbye.

Is there any other choice?
But,
I often wonder...
Who will be unlucky
I who will die
Or you life
Who will be denied
The fullness of life.

DO BE JUST

Break my heart
Break it God
Break it,
If you must.
Break it
In a way
No one should
Get hurt.

My pain I can
Bear it
Yes,
Bear it
With a smile
What I cannot
Bear, is the pain
In their eyes.
Those who love me
And suffer as much.

Break my heart
Break it God
But, please,
Do be just.

SEARCHING FOR ME

Disillusioned
Discouraged
Despair writ
On his face
The doctor
Holds my hand
Not my attention
He retreats
The moment
I catch his glance
He hurriedly
Looks away.
Neither he, nor my daddy
Can fool me no way
It's poor Mom
Who is lost to the world
And relies heavily on God
Little does she realize
I dont even have
A lean chance.

I pity her
And sorry be
For none is there
To share
Her loneliness,
Her pain, and
longing, for
only I know

how she cares.
She'll go about
her life, as
any normal human being
only it will be her form
her soul will be searching . . .
for me.

THE PAIN OF REPENTANCE

you will
at last
need me
want me
sometime
in life.

you will
I'm sure
call out
for me
when
lonesome
some-night.
but, alas!
all you will
find is the . . .
dreary silence.

in tears
with fear
in dread
instead of
love.
you will
wish me
near.
but,
I'm sorry
I'll be by then
long gone
wherefrom
no one
ever returns.

the pain
of
repentance
will soak you
in grief and
guilt, and
endless sorrow
is all that . . .
you will reap.
for all the
heartache
that was mine
because
to me,
you were
unkind.

my eyes though
dull
still flicker
with love.
in them
you will find
yet,
no anger
nor hate.

come, oh! please come!
come and see —
my pitiful sight,
I who once
not so long ago
was your . . .
cherished child.

THE UNERRING STRENGTH

She's a brave woman
brave indeed is she
there's no doubt—
about that. Yet,
I get the jitters
when I think about
the final fare-well.

My heart goes out to her
each time I recall her
youthful days; she slept
beside her brood and not
with her mate.

She was always there
whenever needed or called
out for help, she'd kiss
the wound and heal it
be it a finger or a knee-cap.

I see her wince each time
a needle pricks through me;
I wonder how she'd ever bear
to hand me over to the flames.

When I cry, the tears roll
down from her eyes.
I see the lump moving in
her throat and I fight to
hold my own misery in
thousand folds.

This unerring strength
that my heart possesses,
while learning to endure
does speak much for the
breast that I have suckled
for sure.

WHAT THE STARS FORETELL

When I am sad and lonely,
I watch the stars closely.
Wondering . . .
What do my stars foretell?

My hopes, keep slipping
and rising, with my each
passing sigh!
the game has become too
monotonous as,
time passes by.

Who should I believe?
My stars or
the man made science.

THE CROSS-ROADS OF LIFE

With trepidation
And curiosity
I first took
Few steps.
It was like
A toddler
Who is thrilled
Because
He stood well.

The girl who was
Not so long ago
Full of life and
Fun.
Who could laugh
And cry all too
Soon together
Is now at the
Cross-roads of
Her life.

Her eyes have shed
All the tears she had
The laughter is left
Far behind.
All she remembers now
It's the medicine time.

When this little girl
Remembers
How beautiful life was
She feels overwhelmed
For all that she has lost.

All she is left with is . . .
Cherished memories of
The past.
Memories sprinkled with
Stardust
Which gleam in her dreary
Painful nights
And help to soothe
Her vexed mind.

IN THE STILLNESS OF THE NIGHT

As I tread softly
When I feel
A wee bit strong
My heart goes out
To the days that are gone

I am at a loss
But whom do I
Dare ask
What is it
That ails me
And keeps me thus afar
From all that is
Dear to me my school
My friends my games
And my pets.

In silence I beg
In silence I implore
May be God you will
Hear my woes.

Some times I reflect
At the gone by years
My heart warms up
But my eyes fill with tears.

In the stillness of the night
I reach out to God
Fervently hoping
He would wipe out
The scars
In the hearts of those who love me and
Who will miss me most.

147

YET, ANOTHER DAY

The room is small,
And cell-like.
With death-spelt
All over the wall.
It's suppose to be
An isolation-ward
But in true sense
It's not.
For, as soon as
The lights are turned off
And the nurses rounds are over
Everything wakes up vividly
All around me,
To unfold the treasures
That over the years I've known.

Mother sleeps, (or does she?)
On the floor.
With just a thin Dari,
To keep her from the cold.

Those who come in,
To cheer me, look
Almost dead-inside.
The sea roars,
And cries in vain, for
All those inmates
Who too perhaps await
Their death.
The waves beat on the rocks
And wail aloud until . . .
The wee hours of the dawn.

When the day breaks-in
The hope rises with it.
Yet, another day.
Another meeting,
More pain, more suffering.
The ever-waiting eyes
Will once more be glued
On the door.
Who knows,
Who has the time
For someone
Who is dying.

I'LL FIGHT MY FATE

Ask me not
how I feel
for I feel
I will end-up
the moment
you turn
your back.
I feel
the life
slipping by
I feel the
tide rising
in my eyes,
but I weep not
for fear of
hurting you
my dear ones.
I know it
I feel it
in my bones
you suffer
equally
to watch me
sink
low and low.
My world is
crashing
at my feet
but
I dare not
sound my thoughts
for they then will
weigh you down to

your lowest ebb.
And that's just
what I don't want.
I'd like to see you
smiling
just as I do
even though
death looms
in-view
who cares!!
as long as
I have you
and your smiles
to light up my way
I couldn't care less
for pain, or death.
I'll fight my fate.

UNTIL THEN . . .

Each time
I bid you
A goodbye
A part of
Me
Dies.

The slow
Death
Which is
Gradually
Steadily
And
Determinedly
Approaching
Me
To gather me
Into it's folds.

Until then . . .

I dont know
How many more deaths
I have to die.

ECHOES OF THE PARTING SOUL

The candle
Of my life
Is flickering
To its end.
I do not know
When
My end will come.
I feel sorry
For myself,
True.
But
I also rejoice
For you
My unknown friend
For the light
Of my eyes
Shall be yours,
Shall be yours! . . .
So echoes
My parting soul
And may you
Find friends
As good as mine.
This is my earnest prayer.

NOTHING IS UNIMPORTANT

Does early death come
As a punishment?
Or
Does it come too late,
For those who are tortured
By incurable pain?
Is death really cruel?
Or
Is it merciful?

Why do we shun death?
Haven't we known about death?
Doesn't death follow life?
It sometimes
Over-takes us, and
Sometimes, walks sluggishly
Behind.

Death does bring grief,
Just as any parting does.
Goodbye itself carries
The spark of death.
When you bid goodbye
To a loved one, doesn't it
Bring changes, and adjustments?
Isn't the silence, and
The loneliness disturbing?

Nothing is unimportant
Not even death.

When I see death
Looming-in-view
In these lines
I take my refuge:

"When sickness comes and bids us rest awhile
In some calm pool, beside life's too swift stream,
Why rail at fate, and count ourselves ill used?
'Tis then one's soul awakes, weaves dream on dream."